Japanabandon

Travels in Japan

Andrew Geoffrey Kwabena Moss

First Published: 2023

10 9 8 7 6 5 4 3 2 1

ISBN 978-0-6454326-4-0

Printed & Bound in Australia

Published by RoseyRavelston Books

roseyravelstonbooks.com

Part One – Initial Shocks

On Background

Nyumon Sono Ichi
Sapporo Yuki Matsuri
The Landlord
Travel Plans

On Leaving

The Visa
Fingerprints
On Leaving Cosy Beds
Plane Conversation
Japanabandon

On Arrival

On Arriving at Narita Portal
First Encounters
Furo
Blossom
Futon
Postcards in the Kitchen
Chips & Honey
Unlucky Strikes
Seiyu
Muscle Memory
Cardboard City
Tsudanama
Triumvirate of Outsiders

Part Two – Culture Shocks

Part Three – After Shocks

Part One

–

Initial

Shocks

On Background

Nyumon Sono Ichi

Introduction Part 1

I

Nyumon sono ichi
My finger bobs, buoyed along an inky page
It's print as dark and choppy as North Sea waves
Drilled and parroted by rote,
Sealed in taped lingua phone hope

Press play, the ups and downs of unfamiliar cadence
Release birdsong scales in C90 major
Eardrums twitch to the rhythm, pitch and vibrate

Magnetic coating unravels as I tape each lesson
then send them back in the original packaging
deck to deck sellotape stretches, to recycle cassettes

Anata wa eigo wo hanashimasu ka?
Survival phrases, I play and rehearse on paper
Again, and again I try to nail the perfect intonation,
a parrot trapped in a birdcage language lab

<u>II</u>

Bubble wrapped in the taxi's seats, I use my recipe
Anata wa eigo wo hamashimasu ka?

My experiment falls on deaf ears
White gloved hands grip the steering wheel
Wrapped in misfortune
the driver recoils in fear, nerves edging
the prospect of an English proficiency test

A salutary introductory lesson, nyumon sono ichi.

Sapporo Yuki Matsuri

Icy sculptures on Sesame Street
A winter festival on TV
The Sapporo Yuki Matsuri!
Faraway palaces carved
Ice shavings litter the glass

Years later I slip and zig zag,
mark lines on Hokkaido's
thick ice
a layered
frosted cake, I ride my life on thin ice

How I wish I could skate!
Gripping tight to edged dreams
I hold on fast to childhood memories

The Landlord

The pink feather duster pirouettes,
Mr M minces around his bungalow bedroom,
Pursing his pencil haired philtrum,
his lips syncing to Kenny Rogers as he croons
Soulful asides, how he caught his wife,
with the best man *in flagrante delicto*,
Eulogies to Haydn, his ex-lodger
He swings back to dance like a slalom skier, swooning

footloose and fancy free these days,
betrothed no more, the consummate bachelor,
with a grin he broadcasts how he sows seeds
across the wild Park Street and How Wood fields

to local ladies weak at the knees
at the glint in the sword that he'll unleash
d'Artagnan collecting feathers in his cap,
a cavalier musketeer with a matching moustache
a gemologist
an organist, a shelf-stacker too
my Renaissance man landlord is quite the catch

I rent his boxroom at low-cost Mondays to Fridays
while he works nights stippling supermarket aisles
with produce, I favour this spartan arrangement,
four magnolia walls, a bed and a desk
Where I burn midnight's oil on linguistics and TESOL
exercises
fuelling my resolve to teach abroad, the ultimate of tests

Travel Plans

As I consult classified information,
where will I go on my newly formed adventures?
Red ovals of hope circle deliberations, choice
The world a serrated oyster that tortures
pearls of wisdom locked in a questioning voice

My finger traces a Lonely Planet
as my mind travels to the Czech Republic
mogul skiing braille cobble stones and statues
composers cast in bronze avenues, overtures
along bridges, in late night jazz clubs sipping absinthe
feasting on exotic meals in bistros and brothels

Then my mind crosses chequered histories stuck in ruts
Roughly hewn walled cities and Romany ghettoes
Stone cold mortars cement fear, prejudice without trust
African students left out in the cold, frozen in icy white rust

As I criss-cross the ELT Gazette red,
a yuki matsuri dream flashes before me
and extends.

On Leaving

The Visa

Over the park baize I am confronted by a sight
Sandstone turns to marble, untouched stone sunlight
The blood red dot flutters above the polished columns
Under a watchful Nikkoshi,
gaijin enter the colosseum, fearful foreigners

One is waxed in Barbour for protection,
against Home Counties elements, inclement weathering
a surrogate farmer from Surrey's commuter belt
tight and stiff upper lipped, I imagine a shotgun
and pheasant tucked under either arm
His pinkie signet rings bells of privilege to my alarm
Later, I'll meet Matt, the man in the wax jacket
As our fates collide and crash, like three ladies on a
bracelet

Under the dim dark beams in a Carnaby Street tunnel
Amber lit liquid lights up our path from seat to bar
At our orientation that night, holding jars glassy eyed
we hide behind pint froth, our defences watertight.

Fingerprints

I enter the belly of the blue buttoned beast
My belongings x-rayed through gates threefold
its uniformity shines with glittered mischief
Gutted fish skeletons betray naked greetings
I'm waved on by a hangman with a MET lanyard
Into a labyrinth of corridors darkened
Escorted to the door, the lady sits like Queen Vic
in mourning dress, welding wrought iron 'r's' with
Cockney 'w's'
Her fingers a cathedral spire cradled in anticipation
She rolls my wrist on the inky bed, side to side
In dactylogram lullaby, the print clings to my fingertips
Black squiggles furrow her lily-white visage
Loops, whorls and arches captured in print
Sweat gilded palms surmount friction ridges
She speaks in perfunctory shaded cynicism
I'm just another statistic, catalogued and inked
Under Stasi spotlight her eyes pierce me
Her skin as thin as tissue, white as the anaemic
Addams Family, I rock my finger, indexed in ink
As she holds it in her vice (like) grip
and guides it down for the final time
For a police clearance check, judged as a criminal.

On Leaving Cosy Beds

I'm told not to go, the usual mumbo jumbo
Like the three kings, my neighbours arrive
with their gifts, wrapped up in themselves
they offer precious treasure
oblique warnings thinly disguised
Worn on the sleeves, advice before goodbyes

You can't trust those slanty eyes
Ever thought what lurks beneath those smiles?
Don't be surprised when they stab a katana
in your back. They don't like redheads or blacks
It's more progressive here, watch for attack
Japs prefer blondes, blue eyes, they think it's better
Oh well, there's always the weather!

And oh yeah, beware their kamikaze antics
They're full of trickery, mind their deceptive tactics
Gawd knows what they think,
in fact, come to mention it
I can never tell a Nip from a Chink!

So went the myths and imaginary narratives.

Plane Conversation

Why does she keep pointing to her nose?
An index tip rests on her proboscis
She talks to me, gingerly,
her head dips in deference,
a butterfly nodding in pollen, by nature defenceless

Ocean waves billow below us,
in soft broken Japlish inflected with hope
Gently, her antennae probes, for conversation
We navigate language as tentatively as a boxer on the ropes,
maiden flights of Nihongo and Eigo emerge from her lips
The nose of the plane touches clouds
Propelled, shifting gears across continents of doubt

She watakushi wa's in a waggle dance
leading me to sweet red nectar
Hinomaru treasure, I buzz as we near
honey viscous/ nerves thick with fear

My forefinger forms a bookmark and I listen
My thumb covers the blurb warning in crimson:
fear of redheads and black devils
What should I expect when we hit the ground level?

Japanabandon

Why do we go? Abandoning our homes
We leave a subconscious trail of questions
Snails carrying houses
leaving behind a line of silver treasure
dotted like indigenous paintings
Shells in shock, yet to absorb previous trauma
behind and in front of us, lacking trust
put ourselves to tests, of our own invention
Run away, seek adventure
To prove your pain,
Obsessional exclusions,
out of place
Your safety defaults on its payments.

On Arrival

On Arriving at Narita Portal

We alight at Narita and board
A never-ending conurbation stretching its tentacles,
the silver line drills suction padded civilisation,
its bevelled bit spins and splinters through concrete
jungles scattering sakura flowers, molten metal bubbles,
spit hanami showers in friction

We poke
our snub marigold lined Sobu nose
into welded cement screens
pink popcorn bursts, lit up at the seams,
Fireworks at either side, teleported transportation
Spiralling, satellites replicate, their blueprints never ceasing
In time to the hypnotic clapping train track rhythm,
as it shudders and shuttles us between cities

School girls in gingham check white lipstick in mirrors,
Louis Vitton bags, flip pitchi studded with stickers glittering
Hello Kitty
Glued rūzu sokkusu flatter fake tanned plump calves
Short, pleated skirts and red, black and camel Burberry
scarves
Manga comics embody, a Sonic the hedgehog adjusts
his spiked locks, an anime punk rocker trussed in gakuran,
gold buttons stud his jet-black costume, collars stand to
attention
their sisters ride train carriage waves in sailor fuku costume

as our train changes track there is no looking back,
as we cling to the starship enterprise, a red dot sits on the
horizon
our clammy hands grip the stirrup plastic stalactite
hold on tight, for the adventures of a lifetime
Fighting g-force we shudder through the birth canal
This is Japan.
On ceiling racks kanji ads flap forth and back, in gusts
blurred lines become defined edgily, in haru fresh light.

First Encounters

〒262-0046
千葉県千葉市花見川区
花見川
Hanamigawa
Hanamigawa-ku,   Chiba-shi
Chiba,   262-0046
Japan

Addressed in exotic shock, coded for postal delivery,
Sealed envelopes stamped in the wax of rubbery approval
administered to my system by shock defibrillation,

Elongated kanji and syllabaries, collide and elide
peacock proud lingo stolen by magpies, received pronunciation
left in limbo,
An Englishman's tongue ties, trips and stumbles

We fly over the granite nail filed JR overpass
Unlocked bicycles recline their baskets in diagonal tiredness
in the metal mesh of the dark railway junkyard,

a firework oasis, pink petalled confetti showers the concrete
jungles uplifted in pixilated characters, modified by electronics
to the beep, crack and hatch of hungry pac-man tamagotchis

Neon kanji cacophonies light our silent steps
My head spins, a pachinko ball released from its parlour of regret,
                              its confines
on a new trajectory, along the runway flies the mind

My escort tells me stories of his American corner
where soon he will return, while we pass a diamond
that glitters uncertainty, shaping each blade of grass
Macarthur's legacy swings tubed aluminium and wood
in the park, stitched mitts and pinstripes dance
the pitched ball sits, white lunar Tsukuyomi in the sky

A sensei leads lines of ducks paddling across roads
on our horizon bob and waddle their sunhats in yellow
girls' red, boys' black Randoseru screwed to their backs,

Ladybirds' hardened elytra forewings retract
and protect soft-membrane hindwings for take-off
Delicate insects with itchy wings, preparing for flight

My guide tells me anecdotes, to defrost
rock hard icebergs surface in culture shock, he points
to a telephone kiosk, where he used to play saxophone

Reinforced glass replaces thin waxed paper shoji
I picture him in a vitrine,
a display of gaijin eccentricity
Exotic exhibits locked
in teleportation chambers –
Mine, yours or their thoughts, different only in name?

Furo

My future wonderland puzzles me as I venture up
The view is no Mount Fuji, but
a two-storey warren, a four by two storey gaijin shoebox
The iron stepped rabbit hole leads me to the top,
leaden feet lift

For a moment I grip,
an orange clad balustrade levelled squat
I glance at my neighbours' hutches festooned with clothes
flags wave washed-out surrender along bamboo poles

Outside crouches a white tub topped with a circular hole
Inside, next to the bathtub sits an acrylic beige cubic metre,
Is this a waterproof karaoke machine?
A balance gama act to boil water

I learn to turn
on the seventies' relic in an evening ritual,
Gas hisses and spits at the wall, then I turn on the water,
switch on the gas at the heater, holding down time's dial…

Now it's time to crank up the light, 'til flame flies its pilot
Waiting patiently for the sluice gates to open and bathe me
like a lock keeper at the Grand Union Canal

Blossom

Ephemeral pink pleasure
Lightly glowing, lightening lives,
Lined under Odawaran sakura skies,
One thousand cherry trees burgeon in breeze
One thousand springing dreams

Office workers lay fruitfully
Under Ueno Park blossom reverie,
Lightly petals blow
Sowing seeds of spring

Sake scented skies darken
Illuminated by blushed bulbs on high,

Night-time excited white, pink.

Futon

The mattress teases me, naked on the tatami
Behind lacquered framed paper shutters, it sits
inflated by its ego, puffed up, arrogant but lonely
a second-hand caryard's Michelin Man dances

Baseless arrogance advances, without wooden support
Moshi moshi greets my report, indignation's balloon
rising in intonation, these things are nothing like
the authentic ones they sell in Argos at low cost.

Postcards in the Kitchen

Fusuma shoji divide my entry, layered with washi
Sepia photos and postcards curl up their autumn leaves
Monthly greetings roll up their sleeves in humid rainy
season, (hibernation)
Dad's scenes of windmills, market crosses and canals keep
me company
ease waves of homesickness, tears stuck to tatami

Back in the kitchen I divide and conquer blu-tac
Redistribute blobs on the back like Robin Hood with
precious treasure
cornering four Bostik dots
Epistles dance with cuneiform wit written large in black biro
Cajoling homesickness, laughing at domestic disasters
from home sick counties of commuter dorms green around
the gills
Reports from frontline redbrick terraces and semi-dets
Dunstable ups and downs, white lions roar on Chiltern Hills

Dad adds a closing adage, abstract wisdom for my travels
He signs off in a flourish as I follow in his footsteps,
Travels in West Africa and now Japan,
I stick the latest one up, kneading scant blue resources 'til
its stuck,
in my head forever, your labours in love
to keep us connected, to keep it together.

Chips & Honey

The saucepan thick with yellow viscous liquid
I pour it out of the plastic cannister
listening to its gloopy one-way conversation
Between its soliloquy, the container inhales exhales
I'm happy as a sand boy, an Englishman abroad
Tethered to mad dogs barking their orders in inner voices

I make my way via Makuhari-hongo station
spaghetti junctions tangle in cement sauce
across smoke billowing roads, a lonely Love Hotel,
a UFO anodyne capsule, a burnished airstream bus
lozenged dream
its tarnished portholes blackened by smoky pollution
that we don't dare to swallow, wash down the illusion

At Seiyu I scour the aisles for giant golden vials,
Bubbling champagne to quench my homesick trials
Looking for the familiar glint of amber liquid
Trapped in plastic vitrines stacked side by side,
Terracotta armies trapped in Perspex aspic
Above and below, I search the kanji mysteries

I know I should be feasting on sashimi or maybe basashi
or some other such authentic delicacy
but I simply fancy some good old British chips,
dipped in something vinegary, its piquancy shrill
in my nostrils, some mushy peas or maybe some gravy
seeking headlines wrapped up in soggy newspaper
this brings my tastebuds and a smile to my lips

I wait   at the stove   in   anticipation
As nothing bubbles, I stir and stir vainly
Then I ladle a spud in the deep spoon,
awaiting a taste sensation
To my amazement, its covered   in honey
If I wasn't so hungry for home, it might be funny.

Unlucky Strike

I smoked Lucky Strike in the first few weeks
to ease the culture shock, I absorbed its tar
lining my lungs, casting their long nicotine fingered shadows
then one morning I woke up
and coughed into the tray of charred witchetty grubs
met by a Mount Fuji volcanic eruption
a mushroom Hiroshima atomic cloud
burst ashen waters pregnant with self-destruction

Seiyu

A supermarket stacked for the senses,
My eyes like pachinko balls spin between aisles
Giant Galapagos apples crowned in lattice polystyrene
sit in plastic palanquins, next thing I'm lost, exiled
enthroned in an Atlantis seabed of sashimi
kaleidoscopes on ice and emotions
Free yet suctioned and trapped by new mystery
Mesmerised, pearls stuck on burgundy octopus
Tentacles beckon me.

Muscle Memory

Muscle memory pulses, I pounce to pick it up,
it crumples monochrome to the touch, the doors sigh shut
ink on my fingers
stuck
in a one-way metal tunnel,

I try to read between its leaves, but stumble
in a magical forest
floored by angled offshoots and bamboo boomerang radicals
impenetrable uncut kanji jungles
I can't cut through its inky twigs
black hira - and katakana I can't see through, my tongue is
tied like Excalibur
between a rock, in a hard place
blunt, far from home, without a phrase or book.

Cardboard City

When the hot air bubble bursts
jettisoned salarymen set up their tents
in Ueno, pots and pans their ballast
perfectly dispersed on shades of blue
waterproof ground sheets line the earth
with cerulean and stainless steely memories

In subterranean Shibuya
a house of placards comes crashing
down and not out, cardboard arrangements
painted with rainbows
opening pots of gold
Makeshift cities still glittering

Tsudanama

It's funny as Funabashi what sticks in your head
A visual hook, the tsu of Tsudanama
Curved like the end of a shoe, you look
In full size, not reduced to sokuon, the script that follows
Incomprehensible in a swirl and cut of inky artistry

Mysterious oriental hieroglyphics, make me shift uneasily
Whereas Matt's obsessed by grammar and hiragana
He picks it up fast as chopstick lightning
Deciphering kanji radicals, he chuckles 'Andy!'
as he deliberates visual associations punctuating mnemonics
He reaches a glottal stop at the end of another mirthful line

Tsudanama Station 津田沼駅, our JR Sobu terminus
Passengers await white gloved butlers, pushing
them at rush hour, pressing sardines into metallic marigold cans
In the early days we crane our necks, catching romaji
like fishermen hooked to windowpanes,
glued by bulging fisheye lenses distorting fresh panoramas
opening new sights, centred white,
green kanji and kana either side, reeled in
hook, line and sinker, we are taken in Chiba's arms.

Triumvirate of Outsiders

Matt, David & I
Travelling souls
Jagged jigsaw pieces
Trying to put ourselves together
Cracked shells in shock
Surviving inclement weathering

One adopted, three bullied
Two for being too dark
In Farnham, Portsmouth and Leighton
With Home Counties frustrations,
David froths as he speaks
of what it was to be the Tunisian kid
The one disabled by sable skin

Matt fiddles with his signet ring
in twists around his little finger
Adopted and sent off
to boarding school at all costs
Souls colliding
Now we're united, a triumvirate of outsiders.

Part Two

–

Culture

Shocks

On Being / Acclimatization

Sobu Sen Regular

I'm a Sobu sen regular,
hopping on and off trains in Chiba-Ken
from the Bōsō Hantō to Tsudanama
A peripatetic ELT teacher
riding the JR East JET stream
White gloves push me on rush hour
Lily petalled finger flowers
adrenalin coursing in my neck as I strain
not to miss the Romaji station names

Chiba, Inage then Shin Kemigawa
From ridiculous to familiar, the numbers thinning
the sole gaijin left
gets off at Makuhari-hongo station, exhale and escape
salarymen exude pungent sake
fumes ferment, congested carriages, rest sakura faces
macaque sleep on cold stone sober neighbouring shoulders

refugees from simian izakaya hot springs
after long days at the office, salarymen and OLs
inemuri, sleep whilst present to the chorus of snoring
to white noise, vibrations and shaking soporific
Obaasan, students, ojisan nod off,
Safe in the aluminium cylinders, their protected kinship
villages.

Tall Poppy Syndrome?

The nail
that sticks up,
hammered home in Western
messages
        and adages, yet I see freeta, kogyaru, women
wearing Disney,
  waving Hello Kitty, Japanese rastas and cyber punks
squeeze to share seats
    with geisha on wooden bench platforms or flat Zori
tatami matted feet,
    bound in geta sandals, rub soles and shoulders with
anime characters,
                manga-factured fashions, in turtle games
hammering,

nails that
stick up
in iron bed-
ded
myths.

EFL Lessons

I

I conjugate pointing and nodding,
conjure action verbs around herringbone halls
trailed by toddlers, trailed by their moms
in a total physical response, dutiful daughters and sons

sing song imperatives ordered in chorus
I flash cards to emblazon instruction
Vocabulary by cartoon introduction
In paired dialogue Kindy kids mumble

II

Lower Elementary lessons come next
The textbook 'Let's Go!' accompanied by cassette
Interspersed with questions and interjections
Tamagotchis hatching electronic alarm bells

Keisuke laughs at the gas he's emitted
Days of Doraemon and Pokemon battles
challenges to cram language down young throats
squeaking nests and tapping beaks

Each time they screech the more we feed them
A kaiten conveyor turning heads to heaven
Revolving regurgitated rotating lessons
A Mos Burger break then back on the treadmill

III

Reaching the echelons of Higher Elementary
we brew a sophisticated miso soup
Teachers Notes crammed on the Sobu
The 'Happy House' of characters wave like the Waltons

IV

After the innocent laughter comes
the sullen cold shoulders of Junior High School
Adolescent Pelmanism,
concentration games played cool,
Trawlers go fish for street credibility

Around a rectangular table the taciturn are replaced
by self-conscious giggles
Dressed in navy cardigans and gingham,
behind Burberry barricades muffle see-sawing voices
tribes under parental radars dressed in
loose socks, manga hairdos, designer badged
camels hunching backs, black and red scarves

V

A quick onigiri from the conveni for late afternoon tea
Then onto adult lesson steps, beginner, intermediate,
steadily up the language ladder, second tongues climb rungs
Advanced and proficient, judged by placement tests
A/B dialogues, in rehearsed conversations

Next come the brave, who seek unstructured 'free
con' classes, Keiko's beady fox eyes fix
her nose points to sniff
out grammatical inconsistencies,
a heat seeking missile
Reading pages of Churchill's diaries, desperate to parse
Convoluted sentences and prehistoric tenses, past
from her, that Winston built his own house, for example

Later in the evening Hitoshi wanders in
for a 'make-up lesson',
reddened in his sake scented skin,
dressed in a squid's inky blue suit
head bobbing above the ocean

a lost buoy in a salaryman costume,
lost in the commotion
his heart stabbed
with seppuku voodoo,
a cracked takotsubo pot furrows his brow
trapped by the lapel pin
neatly hammered in, the corporation badge,
seals his disapproval, his coffin

Hitoshi is obsessed by latrines, cheeks flushing alcohol,
A chuckling schoolboy, punctuating his halted English
He points at illustrations from the book he's brought in,
the North Korean long drop, his toilet humour
I force my grin

VI

Kazuhiro, the vet, dissects, picks at the papers
For current affairs and British culture, swooping
at every morsel of detail like a dinner party vulture
Under his wing, one Friday he takes me on a mission
to the matchstick houses of jōkamachi
old Edo city, like Hansel and Gretel we follow
the breadcrumbs left, secreted temples and shrines, mime
artists sail floating worlds, surfing Hokusai tsunami
on a ukiyo-e board, the great wave off Kanagawa, towering
thirty-six views of snow-capped Mount Fuji

kabuki theatres mask Noh dramas for the high
and the low, the remnants of old Edo
along Kawabata's scarlet gangs, fine red entertaining lines,
We navigate Asakusa's narrow backstreet nagaya
dotted with dōjō, dohyo bordered by rice baled straw
We feast on unagi, swimming in a sweet teriyaki sauce.

Asahi Beer Hall Flamme d'Or

Sumida silk flows

Golden flame horizon blows

Star(c)k architecture

Music Trucks

I

Tak-e-yaaaaaaa, sao-da-keeeeeee
hooks and knits its loudspeaker, a loop on my brain
Bamboo seller, bamboo poles, sings
sings the taut voice boxed in
over shamisen strings
selling door to door, poles for laundry
hanging in the air shrill notes

sounds waft past gomi towers
housing digital treasures, denki seihin and terebi
through washi paper shoji sliding doors, billow
curlicues like a Bisto gravy ad, up and down to tatami
lining my nostrils and empty stomach in my apartment

II

Juicy potato music wafts and waxes me hypnotic
The truck's handbrake jerks to a stop at the gomi
Soothing piquant autumnal air with a wintry bite
Like roast coffee caramelises
my nostrils, savouring smells sweet with delight

Autumn leaves roll in on the breeze
In wafts a song, it sings piping hot
Ishi yaki-imo, yaki-imo, yaki-imoooooooo
A needling voice stuck in a vinyl groove
Stone baked potatoes warm my mood,

Baked treasure encased in silver leaf,
rest redolent on hot stone pebbles
then turns to ecclesiastical burgundy
red skin dishevels and shrivels
You unwrap a purple paper jacket
and taste white flesh grown golden

Ice cream van gramophones wind up a dim and distant past
Tootles the Taxi, milk and coal deliveries, float memories,
Kyoko parts her scarlet wine lips and laughs

drags and draws her thoughts on a menthol straw
retracts it like an actor in a gangster movie, casts
smoky halos to trap her ideas, before she translates
Her cheeks hollow in a fleshy hourglass

Laughing, she sings the songs I don't yet know
Tak-e-yaaaaaaa, sao-da-keeeeeee
Ishi yaki-imo, yaki-imo, yaki-imoooooooo

Ready Meal Revelation

Obento atatamemasu ka?
Each evening you supplicate
Your intonation rising to the gods
[okyakusama wa kamisama desu]
As you follow the irasshaimase ascending arpeggio
You smile behind the counter in Rawsons or 7-11
Always the same question

After weeks I am seized by curiosity
My response a *hai, suo desu ne* and nod
a parrot performing in a conveni cage
You smile and bow acceptance with grace
like an acolyte, carry my bento box

brown crispy tonkatsu absorbs yellow yolk
lies next to a bed of rice
sprinkled with salt and black speckled sesame
neatly divided, a dollop of potato salad-
carrot, cucumber, onion and ham
bound by kyuupee mayonehzu.
Shredded cabbage rests beside it,
tomato and snow peas proudly shoot their colours
five lush brushstrokes on the artist's palette

For the first time you genuflect,
Treasure in your gentle hands
and cross the threshold to the dais
into the silver depths, you open the sarcophagus
and make your sacrifice on the plated circle glass
into the depths of the microwave
The electronic gods sound suzu and bonshō bells

In an instant she delivers me to heaven from hell
My palms receive the warm plastic softening
I smell the sweet pork and egg recipe

Finally, my bento box is heated
Fleeting, yet I savour, warm conveni stored memories

/r/, /l/ **Confusion**

/ll/-/r/ confusion. Japanese speakers often cannot distinguish English /r/ from /ll/. They will tend to use a sound which sounds most like an /ll/ to the English listener...

Red lorry, yellow lorry, red lorry, yellow lorry
Drag your tip truck tongue across the roof of the mouth
against your upper teeth at the back, just like that,
push the air around the sides of your mouth
Red lorry, yellow lorry, red lorry, yellow lorry

Red lorry, yellow lorry, red lorry, yellow lorry
See, the perfect alveolar lateral approximant
That's it, press just the tip of your tongue
against the back of your upper teeth
now voice out through your mouth,
If you struggle, curl the sides of your tongue upward.
Perfect, just like that!
Red lorry, yellow lorry, red lorry, yellow lorry

Red lorry, yellow lorry, red lorry, yellow lorry
The tip truck never touches the roof, see
Purse your lips slightly, like me
Curl your tongue and voice out with your mouth
Red lorry, yellow lorry, red lorry, yellow lorry

Red lorry, yellow lorry, red lorry, yellow lorry
See, the perfect alveolar approximant, aided by your tongue!
The tip right behind the ridge behind your teeth,
though be sure it doesn't touch
Perfect! You have made a narrow space
in your mouth through which air flows!

Red lorry, yellow lorry, red lorry, yellow lorry
I pronounce that we've found the problem
fixed the confusion physically,
this is a phonemic dream come true!

Etiquette I

Chopsticks stand erect
Alive in rice beds, spell death
死 s-h-i, death, decease
A thin two-pronged coffin

Tachiyomi

I'm at the local conveni, a sailor lost at sea,
Lost in Bermuda Triangles of onigiri

I'm a DJ, liberating records from seaweed sleeves
    a tiler, tessellating bento boxes silently

    a manga fan, thwarted, in the aisle
sealed out by cellophane

How dare they stop my tachiyomi?
This country is insane!
Such censorship profane!

Green Tea Ceremony

We fly back to Toke station, sky high in elation
Crouched double on tatami, we can hardly kneel
 at the solemn ceremony,

We walk across the dew, removing dust,
wash our hands and mouths at a stone basin above
Summoned to the machiai by a kimono butterfly

Mariko bows silently to receive, offering us small sweets
Next, she bears a silent witness, forensically she checks
utensils for blemishes
Gracefully our host scoops koicha in three heaps

maximising flavour, serves the highest grade for this
occasion
We gaze politely at scrolls,
sagacious advice wrapped in proverbs and quotes

Our host whisks the chasen to the perfect froth
Hand split from single wood,
Dragonflies hover over lotus flowers cast in iron

New beginnings, purity and enlightenment, the tiger
prowls, protecting us, drooling its stripy jowls
Rapidly stirring the bright mossy forest green to a .
perfect paste

She scoops its racing green, mindfully
her dextrous ladling with chashaku, elegant
as an acolyte at an altar snuffing candles

Watch her measure and serve as lightly as bamboo
Delicate as tissue, the green fibrous matcha stew is brewed
We cup our hands around the chawan bowls, reading
braille imperfections, deep in green bubbling leaf seas

We escape the aftershock, flying high as cranes,
One thousand folded paper tales on our way
uplifted by this strange aftertaste.

Golden Egg Testicles

Matt puts two and two eggs together,
two balls in one basket
gasping with excitement like Archimedes
says *'kin tama!'* in elation
to Keisuke, the ika salesman
Fully enunciated in theatrical display,
across the table

Keisuke erupts in laughter, quaking
at the foothills of a verbal disaster
Mirthful at Matt's ballsy attitude
This rude gaijin faux pas
shoulders twitching up and down, they cannot stop
vibrating in the aftershock.

Home

Makuharihongo, Hanamigawa ku
Perfumed prefectures, scents we never knew
Sakura fireworks light up the smoggy sky
Signs light up, scrupe and scrape the night
Bosozuku vibrate the mantle of your dreams
Catch the blossoming before it's no longer seen
Across Shibuya crossings, in zebra black and white
Metal cannister of hot coffee drop
Vending machines for the lonely and the lost
Through concrete jungle tunnels, savannah summer parks
Skewer seppuku swords, piercing your heart
Magical journeys darkness into light.

Acclimatization

Paranoia sharpens my ears
A fox *fearful*, as I listen to phrases, parsing
time and words in a rainy season,
the clouds above me pregnant with deliberation
until I recognise '*O tenki des(u) ne!*'
Slate skies brighten as I awaken to mundane
conversation
It is a good day today!
Weathering the storm,
acclimatization.

Dumplings for Mum

On an Odawara Odyssey, foraging dumplings for mum
She runs at the electronic sluice gates, cringed at by her son
Like a bullet, shinkansen transports us beyond and above,
The castle lifts and licks its portcullis lips, jaw and yawns
wide like the wooden horse of Troy
a pink petalled avenue lined with a thousand sakura trees,
lead us through a tunnel of dreams

We ride the undulating waves, surf a rickety mountain train
through tubes of bamboo, shooting its scaffold to heaven
Senses sweetened by elongated sugary canes
Arriving at a wooden shack, kanji flags flutter on canvas
I rehearse phrasebook sayings, gyoza incantations
Satiate our prayers, interpret my intonation

Mists whispers linger whispering in volcanic valleys
Owakudani hell vents anger as black eggs boil sulphuric
waters
Below Dad rows, oars spread wings in ripples
diamonds twinkle whilst mirror images flash the caldera,
the crater lake opens the aperture
Moments snapped capture our hearts forevermore.

Etiquette II

Acute attention, angles bowing
Become reflex reactions to greetings
Misunderstood handshakes, roughly obtuse
The delicate meishi drama unravels slick moves
Long eared lapins, rabbits pulled out of wallets
By magicians wearing business suits
Receive hidden messages guarded by kanji sentinels

Moshi moshi Edo rituals
Humbly wait on the line, biding honorific time
Making sure kitsune won't shapeshift
Self-sacrifice for guests,
Okyakusama wa kamisama desu
Expressions lie prostrate, stretched out in respect

Exchange slippers at the front door of the bathroom
Shower before ofuro
When you sneeze, never use a bata kusai
handkerchief,
And beg repentance
Etiquette your second good nature
Your new seventh sense.

Chiba Shi Station

In fuyu mountain air, high in Peruvian altitude
pan pipes chime in poncho duffel coats
Woollen rainbow chevrons point downwards
Eagles circle CD piled mountains
Quencha qina flutes sound in the train track valleys

We follow the signs and arrows,
In orderly Edwardian preppy fashions
Kogal boys dressed toe to head in overcoats
Fur lined boa collars constrict and clutch
Hello Kitty stickers glitter on Louis Vuitton handbags

Tubes and ribbed loose socks grip to solarium brown legs
Deep ganguro tans clash with metallic bleached locks
Manga fashioning flatters plump calves after birthed
Fresh from magazines in conveni racks
Dressed in gingham miniskirt shades of blue

Beige, red and black fashion tragics, noosed
in Burberry scarves, hook links in necklace chain arms
Mitsukoshi and Takashimaya bags
Striped glossy in rainbow TV test cards
energetic schoolboys rush on trains and advance

their hair gel sculpting their cheekbones
Gakuran black ants cling onto silver leaves
Black suits and gold buttons blush in sunlight
California Valley girls wash up on platforms
Surfing portals, transported by fashion currents

Solid base tans and bleached blonde Baywatch
Look across for romantic Davids without Hasselhoffs
Agejo hostesses foxtrot in fur lined coats
Cute hime gyaru dolls line up by shops, hooked
arm in arm link with their gyaru-o boyband counterparts

Prepped American casuals, skate the polished ice floors
Peacocks dressed in cardigans, slacks and penny loafers
adjust their Alice bands and check tans in train mirror
doors
Shining reflections, Zen emptiness or freeter existence?

Vending Machines

South Korean won drop
Holed and drilled in diamond precision
Watch the green tea and coffee cans descend
Cold metal cannisters in your hands
White spirit joy
A One Cup sake bottle thuds to the floor
A ghostly vision sent from the vending machine
Treasures found are treasures spent.

Harajuku Salon – Instant Dread

They laugh as they surround me
'Formuru U-One' they quip
tongues flexing the whip with Japlish mischief
Crochet needles from Tokyu hands grip
And weave my nappy head into instant dreads

I'm shown three widths to choose from, threads
nailed to a block of rustic wood
The artisanal mirror beams my image
sitting on the salon palanquin
okyakusama wa kamisama desu
The customer is King

Many salon hands loop my roots
like the laces of a shoe, making a base
the silver woodpecker wefts the needle
up and down by backcombed afro
No need for a yakuza perm first they joke
Concrete dreads form instantly in a Harajuku jungle.

Hokkaido

Ice thickly layered on skidding streets
Slip and catch your icy breath, your red heartbeat
Gliding Sapporo's post-war gridded floor

We eat fresh melon and pull crabs legs
Tender white-pink fresh flesh
Then we head to Russian churches
clad steeple minarets, stippled thimbles protecting
needles

A sailor drowning in stubble mumbles 'spacebo'
as he fumbles for loose change
a few miles from the Hokkaido-Sakhalin divide
a Kuril island chained between disputed nations.

Strange Train Junctions

The Go player from Romania reclines,
then suddenly his eyes in a grandmaster flash
advance on a Mobara line in abstract art,
he starts a conversation
our eyes lock acknowledgement's antlers -
travelling gaijin grown lonely, our radar lights,
up mirrored in estrangement
as we bob up and down the Boso-Hanto
surfing the twisted metal waves

we engage displaced tongues in a rich storytelling exchange
An artist from a floating world unfurls his tales
rolling time capsules woven on makisu mats
We talk of Ceauşescu's orphans, lost in cradles
Souls caught in slaughterhouses, rocking
to the beat of trauma
We take a trip to the plight of the Romany

Gypsies walled in ghettoed cities
Flower sellers wipe saliva from their faces
playing second fiddle to the baying crowds
Up to fanged Dracula mountains, tips drip
icy snow pitched Gothic castles sit,
our minds shift swiftly as a rally gearstick

The Go player and I, snug under kotatsu
Comforted by our izakaya tales
Thawed by imaginings, settle like snowflakes
into our newly found surroundings

Asking for Directions

Lost, they guide me, at their side
Virgils travelling in foreign moccasins
Sensible salaryman black shoes tap dance,
Spat out and polished, soles worn down yet
they acquiesce to my requests,
Geta sandals sink in tatami
Down to earth with a soft landing
The gaijin guiding feet that steady me.

Tokyo Tokyo

Akihabara
Abracadabara
Electric circuitous circus of magic
Neon pollution
Twenty-four, seven-eleven convenience stores
Electronic Revelations and revolutions
Light up the confusion
Confucius says, 'It's not the way…
to spiritual enlightenment'
As East meets West

Harajuku jukeboxes
Play Elvis
Cultures collide and embrace
Streets parade
In the east facing west
Seamlessly
In Evisu denim shades
Quiffs rock and roll
Blowing in sakura scented breeze
Backed by a rising sun
West meets East

Hanamigawa-ku salarymen swing imaginary irons
Brief cases fly high
Pink glow
In an ink black night

High above electric cables
of commuter railway stations
Cherry blossoms and fall
On a Sobu-line train
Paranoia hones the ears
to expat fears of being *gaijin*
Japlish jabbering
Stuccatoed vowel hammering
Salarymen slobbering
Noodle stand slurping
As a sake face tinged red
the bittersweet stench lingers fermented
then sleeps on your shoulder
flying over
on the Sobu-sen sobering.

Bonsai

My tiny gift, I diligently water it
Watch its twisted metal limbs
Spiralling, grafted gnarly skin
It sits in its ceramic cerulean petri dish
This delicate experiment of temperament, shifting
Feng shui lotus positioning,
I balance yin and yang like a yogi on a mat
Enough shade and sun on the balcony
Scales balancing fate, contriving nature's way
Capability Brown
I fill it with love to the brim
until it withers, leaves
drop and die
in
my fingers
ephemeral as Samurai

Pontocho

Atmospheric alley ways reverberate
Shijo to Sanjo-dori ancient rites tunnel passageways

through powdered geisha conversation
Ceramic okiya bowls clink, mix matcha bamboo tools

that whisk tea green leaves, bubble in cauldrons deep
Apprentice maiko tug magical shamisen strings

Sing shrill kouta, tightly pulled kimono bows at bridges
mask salmon sake faces, boxed in kabuki drama

Artists of floating worlds struggle against currents
upstream
Koinoburi banners flutter their flags in giddy happiness

Karaoke confusion and salarymen zig zag movements
Bamboo forests grow elongated sugar cane antennae

Extending telescopes reach their scaffold to the sun,
bittersweet memories' tentacles reach heavens above

Bonita flakes curl and dance next to hot octopus
Takoyaki, paper thin fish shavings shimmy and shine

While udon chefs slice fates into noodle string filigree
We, the slivers under knives of clock faced needles

Christmas in Japan

I'm dreaming of a white Christmas
Lyrics I cut up and we jigsaw-ed back together
Dada free word associations,
Messages underwritten in oblique homesickness blues
We put the pieces back
Neatly rearranging myths to fit our heaven
fictions to fit our facts

Chiba crisp fuku air drops its flaky mana
on homeland memories reimagined in trust
Where grass is always greener
The snow is whiter and doesn't turn to slush

We clutch to crackers, before the joke explodes
and bursts our false economy of chuckling bubbles and
hope
baubels and tinsel, turkey trimmings, stockings brim at the
seams
Childhood yuletide clogs our dammed dreams
We carol sing for figgy pudding on the high street
and sugar dusted mince pies, fillings so sweet

We organise their games, kids race in relays
to pick up Smarties with slippery plastic chopsticks they
rush
Blindfolded, we spin them like tops
Pinning tails and hopes on Mary and Joseph's donkey
Santa and Rudolph's red shiny noses

Bing continues as we pull cylinders stocked with treasure
Shattering into parts of speech, idioms demand our parsing
as the Advent calendar chimes us closer to pleasure
At lesson end, we are showered by gifts from kings
and queens, golden cufflinks, frankincense, Bulgari
aftershave,
Burberry scarves wrap up our muffled mirthful laughter
On our way down the elevator we frown, could this be
Christmas in Japan?

Sampling Food in the Sky

From the scuba-diving basement we elevate
The brush steel curtains widen
A polished top floor, sparkles
a marble department in the sky
Chopsticks clink against bowls

Dimpled moons reach the skies
A satisfying thwack and smacking lips
Salarymen drive iron with full swinging hips
Clubs whip the air, nets protect
pedestrians, ants crossing zebras

Models bow serried on shelves
replicas dressed in plastic, wax and resin
shine under paparazzi lamps
tempting tourists, balancing
aesthetics and realism, the *shokuhiru sampuru*

Mannequin dishes next to food model bowls
help us to navigate, poured from wax to plastic
silicon moulds fill and whet our appetites
Iwasaki omelettes fashioned from melted candles
Each grain of rice painted by hand.

What the Dickens?

Ebisu expat revellers spill in and out
Drinks arc tables to mouths

A Russian bodybuilder bursts
at the seams
His monobrow furrows,

Tense tremors before us, we see
a testosterone explosion
In aftershock we retreat

Drink to release us from hard times
the daily grad grind
loosened lips lubricated with quips

Artful dodgers pickpocketing cultures
Hybrid gaijin gabble in Japlish
In the bleak public house, travels unravelling.

Train Station Facades

Across the way, lies
a parallel universe

Parked in a valley between the rails
in between the metal scales of JR and Keisei Shin trains

Kaihin Makuhari skyscrapers wink their sore eyes
Red eyed flights in the pin drop silent starry skies
Warning signs to landing UFOs and love hotel makers
Perfect strangers in surreal lunarscapes

Nikuman

Nestled among Ginza's silver guilds and gilded treasure
caskets
lies a jewel tucked under the concrete jungle, it sits
comfortably plump
modest, yet its chest puffs up in a cross hatched basket
From Sino-seas, the chukaman chugs on silky watery roads
in bamboo steamers concealing its passengers of many
fillings, fluffy and soft
clouds outside the judgement, paddles raise the perfect
ten in winter season
buy them by the dozen, their folded spiral fractals twinkle
folded like picnic boxes in cherry blossom blankets,
right hand thumbs fold edges counter-clockwise, moving
slowly
bubble gum lunar buns, igloos housing pork, shiitake
mushrooms,
cabbage and scallion, wintry Chinese warmers in the
waning sun

Uyoku Dantai Vans

Military music perforates the air,
a horn section polishes the molecules as a gang
is about to burst and bustle from the gaisensha van,
Hinomaru emblazons their canvassing

Like the A-Team about to jump out of a plane,
parachute cords in hand, to the baton
of a marching band, the Kimigayo brass
plays hide and seek with shamisen
I see their bomber jacketed and aviator-ed silhouettes
their frowns are covered by hachimachi headbands
behind the double tinted windows

A dystopian ice cream van has landed
Its wound-up gramophone in rage, distorts the airwaves
Beware gaijin, out they jump onto the pavement
Loudspeakers blast, fastened and project
the two-winged praying mantis
rubs shoulders, wingbacks to backs, its
sonic antennae facing forward

My eyes are drawn to the driver's door
Luring me like a bee to the odour of chrysanthemums
The sixteen petalled kikunogomon
wafts in the air, poisonous as deadly nightshade
imperially sealing hybrid fate
What would they make of me?
A brown face in a yellow sea.

PHS

My pitchi flipped, open limbed sophistication
This is no Nokia brick, read my lips
'Summimasen, I've got to take it,'
A killer whale's glossy jaws,
a polished Venus fly fishing trap

my jet black, obsidian
rectangular talisman catching me in its prism
An electronic gymnast doing the splits
One hundred and eighty degrees
In black lycra leotard
Japanese technology
Designed for nimble fingers
'Moshi moshi…'

Tokyo Tan(g)ka

Sakura
Scented skies
Burgeoning bright blossom
Pink fluffy popcorn explodes
Entertaining film spools out joy

Revealed golden orb, dry heat
After sulky overcast skies
Rain ripened plums
Six weeks
Tsuyu

Mommiji
Rain, wind
Burnished by sun,
Bruised burgundy, brown golden
Pot pourri basket of leaves

Offerings of heavenly, flaky manna
Turned grey white al fresco
Blue Sistine firmament
Refreshing crisp
Yuki

Sakura – cherry blossom
Tsuyu – rainy season, literally plum rain as it coincides
with ripening plums
Yuki – winter or lucky

Textbook Citizen

To John and Liz Soars, authors of the Headway English Language Teaching resources

I came to Japan without the highspeed JET programme
nor by shin-kan-sen
Instead on a lowly Boeing 447
I Soared in the sky with John and Liz –
my teaching guides –
    Beginner, Intermediate, Advanced
making Headway – but never proficient
in Japanese nor English.

At Harajuku Market

An orange flame haired Turk
lifts the curtain, revealing clothes on racks
Cannabis leaves, Marley and Karl Kani
hip hop hoodies heaped on a Kali Mountain
tags and hangers strewn at the ground
His copper penny freckles join
jagged dots across his forehead

He barters in staccato stepped pidgin Japlish
to his Ghanaian mate dreaded natty
as customers pick, fleas at the market
Parasites at capitalism's carcass
Gifts of the gabbling Babel,
a confusion of spirited tongues
Everyone on their travels, searching for Zion.

Earthquake

So, I'm in the kitchen making a cuppa
  dipping a green tea bag when
    things start to shake, a gentle baby rattle
      then a thicker corrugation
        like travelling outback west, on the plains
          across the Nullarbor, or St. George's Ranges

    Anyway, the ceramic plates, tectonic, on the mantel
      shake and fall with my jaw on the floor
    The cupboard half open swings in invitation
  to join the rumbling chorus, and drops cups at once
bowls and plates downward drip in gravity's hastening

I'm on the road one day and suddenly
 It moves, it slopes right under my feet,
   A gentle reminder
     I look down at my instep edge, a shudder down my spine
       The tremors on my Richter Scale subside.

Bōsōzoku Blowing My Mind

Hear the roar of the Bōsōzoku
Revving their engines, the bajutsu
Samurai on electronic horseback,
Tracksuited in Gyōtoku night
Shoals schooled in cool bitumen bite
fish rumble in time with the Tozai blue line

pause, a pregnant purr   before the next roar
pricking the silver stippled sky as it darkens
grease lightning lubricates my mind
Gelled back rockers and mods camouflaged in parkas
throttle and con my thoughts
Thieves in the night whom I heard but never saw.

Evisu Jeans & Sukajan

In (the) deepest darkest denimed indigo dreams
Two V signs in rebellion fly at the back, across the seams
Designer doves paint-splashing pockets of peace
Their curved wings a Hokusai white flag waves
a jean pool engraved in ukiyo-e paint

Above shimmer sukajan jackets in harmony
A balancing act with yin and yang
embroidering national myths and memories
Chrysanthemum, crouching tigers and cranes
softened by willow and sakura, float in divine breeze

Kyoko's Ryōshin

They let me in, enveloping
       Broad mandarin countenances
Kyoko, Keisuke and Kanako, segments
in a family. My pith sticks between them
long enough to be welcomed in

Cherry Blossom Rain

Shoegazing in Ueno, head down looking at the brown edged petals

Cherry blossom rains on the boy from South Beds,

after the stormy downpour, remembering

the Hockliffe Road snow that turned to yellow,

then fermented brown to polluted black

trodden down in Leighton's rush hour commotion

How strange this cherry blossom snow

How strange these flurries of the imagination

these blizzards that freeze emotion

How strange these light showers of fate ephemeral.

Blossoming To(ward) Death

The cherry blossom's gossamer silken stream gathers
consciousness, transiently fleeting like the pirouette
of a Fenland skater on thin ice, as the scrupe of kimono
drifts
offering Death's reminder for the way of warriors, ready
in final contemplation
utter Bushido in a short last breath
five sided blossoms, thin as paper traced and left.

Ode to O-nigiri お握り; 御握り; おにぎり

Oh O-nigiri,
Japanese roulette, triangular destiny
Elliptical white rice頓食 wrapped in salty *nori* 海苔
Green, black flecked sparkle meets my eyes
Air and fire point to Father Firmament
Ground and water to Mother Earth
Trinity, Third Eye watching over
Strong base, immense support
Seven-to-Eleven conveniently stored
Fitting Heian plates, lining the shelves

I unwrap your cellophane tentatively
Following the 1,2,3 ritual unveiling onigiri
Rice separated from seaweed with sheet thin plastic
Preventing *gohan* ご飯going soggy
Following the prompts on your packaging
Three equilaterally important steps:

1. Pull the middle strip down, all the way around to the back
2. Gently remove the right sleeve
3. Then with the left, repeat

O-nigiri revealed ready to eat

I hesitate, mouth poised in limbo, I salivate
Awaiting the fateful taste
Pausing to consider your illustrious history
Oh O-nigiri, my triangular destiny
Carbon imprinted fingers on grains since times of *Yayoi* 弥生時代

300BCE to 300CE
Travellers moulded you into Shinto mountains
Scaling scalene geometrical trajectories
Seeking protection from *kami* 神
I seek providence for my choice

What will you bring? Salvation or disappointment?
Oh O-nigiri, filling me with your mystery
Takuan 沢庵 pickled radish or *tarako* 鱈子 salted cod roe
Shirasu 白子 whitebait or *okaka* おかかのおにぎり
moistened with soy sauce, dried bonita flakes
Umeboshi 梅干 pickled plum or *sake* 鮭おにぎり salted
salmon or *yaki* 焼きおにぎり grilled
Kombu 軍布 simmered seaweed or tuna mayonnaise
O-nigiri, I pray
On this occasion what will you offer?
I dodge the *umeboshi* plum stone cosh
If only I read *kanji* 漢字 I wouldn't be lost
Oh O-nigiri, Japanese roulette, triangular destiny.

Macaques Mirrors

In the magical looking glass Old World monkeys attract us
Nihonzaru native terrestrials painted in pink make up
Whilst the steam rises from Hell's Valley hot springing cracks
Young cousins dip in rotenburo whilst geriatrics do
backstroke
down evolutionary laddered rungs they hold tight

A troop of matrilines and youngers groom
We look at a mirror, our neurons fire, soon sound their
harmony
Bathing and rolling snowballs, their opus movement
Gathering momentum, our premotor cortex takes off
In chorus, illusions between observers and actors narrow

See no evil, hear no evil, speak no evil, before us
Mythical Raijū keep company for lightning gods
After them, we mindread narratives to survive
Our drive to tell stories of snowy monkeys' minds.

The Illogical Progressions – Lab Rats in Roppongi

Bukem bends down low, his walnut shaven head aglow and
deferent,
An escapologist, Buddhist mendicant
Freed from shackled Watford shopping precinct land,
he pipettes musical medicine, hypnotic chemicals in
reverence
His aspergillum finger points skywards so we lift our hands
Dotting Honshu with a flight case, we imagine him
From a silver Good Lookin' Records bag, he whips them
out
like a magician pulling rare bit grooves from a hat
Legendary LTJ, we abbreviate and chant his name, his
moniker

An alchemist dipping his fingers in Akan pots of gold
He's big bug eyed, Buddy Holly goggled and magnified
An oversized Jeff Goldblum from Jurassic time
Bono's Fly on the wall is camouflaged in the dark
The white coated scientist operates, scalpel ready on vinyl
Aligned, he's silhouetted against a blue neon aquarium
a splashback dais pulses whilst Roppongi gleams
One ear to steel ribbed platter's bevelled edge, he listens
in

a diligent doctor hovering with a stethoscope
alert to the faintest of ground-breaking tremoring,
the other cues in concentrated narrowing,
to divine the perfect beat match to BPM
Darting across from side to side in a tennis game of snap,
eyes glued to the monitor, our pilot equalizes graphically

Levels' rectangular slabs of colour rise up and down
Cat's eyes against the night's background, hear the sound

Looping line graphs chart our memories
we ebb and flow with the waveform's fluorescent scenery
rumble fish on black and white and silver sheen
Drum and bass ensnare us suddenly, rattlesnakes slither
An anaconda squeezing and swallowing
down our backs and necking bittersweet ecstasy,
with verve our minds hum in time with these symphonies
A priest answering prayers answering worries

In his confessional DJ booth, dressed in a white T-shirt
cotta
beneath a double denimed cassock, the cowboy rides his
range
spinneret records holstered, an Anansi shooting silky
strings
from carapace, our Rainbow Serpent, our Dreaming grace
Mesmerising charms float in the breeze, the crystals chime
as rare grooves mix with acidic jazz, made alkaline
psychedelic wah wah pedals trip in time with keyboards,
vocals align as we feast at a sakura illuminated picnic

Orchestral jams for Japan's jungle fans, the fire
A logical mystic in crime, to his right, MC Conrad holds
tight
the Pentecostal microphone, preaches and toasts a bass
drum gospel
Boldly aloft a lyrical ladder, larynx rising up to meet the
disco ball, he climbs
Shining syllabaries sweep us up on a sonic journey
Our shaman between places and time signatures translates
a magical odyssey of remembrance, we jump to embrace
our fate
and touch muscular memories crepuscular at dusk

Endorphins pulsate and release deepest reveries
As we move on and as we progress an invitation extends:
To jump back and kiss the sky for the rhythm
Increase the pleasure and ease the stress
Conrad exhorts our passive willingness
You move your body, and we'll do the rest
We pause for breath and contemplate our empty shells
Filled for a moment of hope, we join the crescendo.

Kyoto Tanka Triptych
Kinkaku-ji

Bamboo forests shoot

Kinkaku-ji floats, golden

lotus reflection

pagoda wings stretch and fly

Ryōan-ji

Dry landscaped rock, pools
within clay-stained rusty walls
Moon safaris rake
Polished riverbeds unspool

Saihō-ji

Stagnant lily pads
Heart shaped islands sham rock
one hundred shades green
Kokedera velvet moss
Flooded in a virid sea

Fashioned Tribes / Kei

Yoyogi rollers shoulders rub with Takeshita Dori hordes
Kei armies march
in shopping malls and strips
Zoki hairlines recede. Bullied into thinning quiffs
Polka dot skirts open their bike spoke parasols
Scarlet Harringtons spin in indigo ink,
turned up juke boxes and denim, Laced by
Grimm Anderson dreams, hobbles crooked Little Bo Peep
Grimoire trussed in ye olde velvets
drip silky embroidery
Dolls on the border of Harajuku/ Shibuya streets
Lolita Kei in riots of pink,
drink their Molotovs
Drunk on a fairyland fantasy, frilled at the edges
A cocktail mixes aprons, pontiff's crosiers and bonnets
We follow the procession led on by the shepherd
Gosurori goths ink their predecessors black
Harajuku jukeboxes spin visual kei and hair metal bands
Applied snow white make up to match
Glay and L'Arc En Ciel mascara hides
cross pollinated anger
A sound clash with accessories mismatched
in abandon
Hodgepodge Harajuku
breeding kei, Tokyo tribes
From Takeshita to the catwalks purr, lap it up, unite

Etiquette III

Summimasen
Oops, I did it again
      Britney speared the chopsticks
in her bed of rice
and made for herself a bed of nails
An etiquette slip up wouldn't suffice
her manager warned her
As the paparazzi flashed and dazzled
The downtown noodle barred,
its slurping chorus rang before them
Conducted by hashi baton
Accompanied by Udon chopping woodwind
Yet this faux pas would not restrict her
            progress up the
            ladder of rice
            paddy terrace
            To stardom
            Britney was
            the heiress

Yokohama

A meal overlooking Yokohama's containers,
Freight stacked like shoe-boxed parcels
Picked up by crane's pincers. Lifted
by distal and middle phalanx, a thumb
and index finger grip corrugations in unison
A Christmas Day freed from conventions
I taste the sweet Chinese cabbage leaves
Light green and sugar coated, memories
Buddhist, Shinto and Catholic syncretic celebrations
Freedom from being stuffed on heavy turkey trimmings,
brussels sprout out of control and cranberry, faces full
to the brim with carbohydrates. Light fluffy rice
lifts me up cloud nine destined in this festive seasoning
Reinventing the Dharmic fortune wheel
that I used to be chained and strapped to.

Genki

Ikana genki des(u) ka? いかがですか
O-genki des(u) ka? お元気ですか
       Genki des(u) ne. Lively untranslatable
           Brave faced strength covered in dust at
the chalk face,
              against the blackboard, against
shame
                This positive attitude
brought to the classroom
Energetic, lively cajoler, leader with grammatical rules
lined behind followers unspool, deferent to the oracle:
the open question conversation instigator, eternal
interrogator
smiles broadly to encourage a love of the language,
a language of love, load up
on our cultural baggage too, o-kyaksama hooked by lively
taiken
demonstrations, a genki sensei is everybody's saviour.

The Swiss Fondue Set

We eat from a glacial landscaped lake, harboured
deep in a cheese fountain
                            and discuss the topography of topical
ranges in alpine mountain airs,
                            say our graces *itadakimasu*, a
Japanese student,
and her Swiss hippy husband, locks encircled, high on
altitude
girdled by a Björn Borg headband, both scientists who
met in Ghent
then headed to Geneva for conventional holy
matrimony. We sit,
mismatched misfits in a white crystal Lego block,
stacked against the odds –
a capitalist communism,
a diffusion of wealth,
trickling down drizzling
from rainclouds.
We discuss low crime
rates, peace
and middle
classes
monolithic.

The Wolves of Nikko Forest

Filigree forests dapple mossy spotlights
Strip bark and gobble, alpine flowers, crops
Trampled by the antlered

Packs are called to quell the menace
Set loose and deep in ravines
It's time to reintroduce fairy tales Grimm

Or is this human tinkering?
Forests crossed with highways, dotted
Dwellings, ski slopes and golf course baize

A haven for those clothed in fleece
Should they be our neighbours?

Umbrella Terms

In rainy seasons out they pop
The easily obtainable, disposable saviours
Grant us transparent delivery
As we negotiate dense bodied
concrete forest streets, in full visibility
under sudden cathartic skies
Mi kasa es tu kasa, we lend and borrow
Contract the flimsy spikes and slide
Encase it in the condom sheathed dispenser
Long and slender, catching drops
Now you are ready to enter.

Mommiji Moment

Burnished green, brown, red

    Hang sweetly their leaves

        Maples burn syrup in trees

Inter-seismic Identity Slippage

Inter-seismic slips, accumulate
As the needle ticks
Vacillate the metronome, measure home
The elastic strain of not being English
or Ghanaian, obibini nor obroni
Pulled by first and third world problems
The Global north and south
shadow my inner compass

Over and under sights, it's time
to expose my fault lines
frictional locking identity, penetrates
every waking night and day
calcifies my brittle childhood bones
sticks and stones thrown from the green housed
Elastic strains in tension far from home

So, it's time for an alternative adventure
Test tubular thought experiments
ring their alarm bells in your head
In peals of nervous laughter
You travel in fear's direction
Shed the aegis, shed thick skinned protection
Headlong to a third space
Shrouded in another splendid isolation.

Part Three

–

After

Shocks

Post-seismic Slippage

When you ride your bike in the rain,
covering the brakes, knuckle white
in the self-protection
holding an umbrella in your left grip
they raise their eyelids, that's post-seismic slippage

When you bow in reflex on entering and leaving
a shop, greeting friends and acquaintances
in differing degrees, that's post-seismic slippage

When you enter Lake Street's Golden Lotus,
next to that Baptist's organ pipes
where, as a boy, you sang all things beautiful and bright

After lubricating at The Golden Bell,
you argue at all costs
at the lack of a bow or irasshaimase

or high-pitched smile
You argue the spin and toss of a coin,
the disappointment of it all, that's post-seismic slippage

you forget your own currency
in a hurry you miss the holes in the middle
a Queen usurps Natsume Sōseki

gone the 1,000 navy blue novelty,
left lost at sea without Tsuda on 5,000
or Yukichi's 10,000 leagues underneath

Left to drown in memories, you apologise

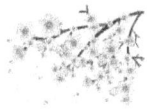

Summimasen and bow, drop your anchored yen and yearn
now weighed down by the pounds you earn
Met by frowns, that's post-seismic slippage

Order numbers serve to annoy the gruff bingo call
in the foyer, let your elbow rest in recompense on formica
bench
no longer o kyaku-sama wa kami sama desu

Denied at the tori, you drop your head
in polystyrene crackers poisoned prawn
and dream of sake and sashimi, that's post-seismic slippage

You go home and turn on the TV,
expecting tarentos on terebi
no garish jumpers greet your eyes, you sigh instead

In time for the despair and gloom
of current affairs, cemented in establishment
broadcast from BBC news roomed doom

But the next week you see a hundred welcomes
black on a whitewashed wall indelibly scrawled
Welcomed at Salusbury Primary:
Akwaaba, Haari Mae, Witaj
you feel at home in aftershock, absorbed once more.

Ainu Rebels

Ainu Rebels dance, robed in ancient movements
Clothed in remixed language, hip hop, rap step out the
shadows
Resurrect for extinction's brink, a truth

Let out the hiss of stereotyped pressure
No longer on the edges, no longer held to ransom
Sing your songs from the brink of extinction

Uncover from samurai shielded homogeneity
The island cul-de-sac cut off its indigenous
Dig for the treasured Jomon-jin remnants in gaiety

Hunting and gathering clues, find the OG descendants
Merge Okhotsk and Sastumon, the children of the sun
Long rays of hair, full beards and tattooed mouths

speak of coming to adulthood, rites of passage
Bow and arrow shoot with poisoned spear
Fox, bear and deer coming nearer

In solemn Iotame bear the head of gods
Raised young cubs gambol like Ainu children
Sacrifice, release the kamuy spirit within

Bless the Kim-un Kamuy,
Bless gods of bears and mountains.

Stereotypes

Lullaby babies and ladies ululate the Tales of Genji
In moss gardens weave Zen gentle artistry
Courtiers descend delicate as dew morning's tapestry

Seppuku skewered samurai, arrogant, punctilious
punctured victims embalmed in feudal pyramids,
rule bound and mummified in Tokugawa systems

Militarists lead by brutal conquest Asian tigers,
dragon slaying animals, stripped in single mindedness
ruthless kamikaze sacrifice, ephemeral sakura leaves.

Timelines

I contrast the present, perfect
  with the past, etched on a linear track,
  without complex webs, connections
  a simple timeline forth and back
  marked in whiteboard pens'
  cylindrical time capsule test tube
  Brainstorms, thought showers and mind maps

I differentiate between worlds in intervals
  fly in my time machine of finished and unfinished
  symphonies, follow my time signatures –
  galaxies to travel today perfect and back past
  to yesterday at different stages on a yardstick

Memories past and present perfect
  sketch themselves in my brain's pages
  My synapses fire across spaghetti junctions
  neural pathways lead to nirvana, this must be karma.

Grand Slam Shockwaves

Osaka smashes flushing meadows blue
to blush red clay anger in embarrassed hues

feel the reverberations from a hyphen-nation
Japanese- American Haitian-

A grand slam on a righteous Richter scale
Haafu pseudo-races expose the fissures

on double fault lines, umpired empires crumble,
tectonic plates separating nations shift

No longer uncomfortable in opposition
but in glorious combination no more humbled,

game, set and match in hybrid heaven
Stand in ovation to Hinomaru in Haitian Revolution

Three-hundred-and-sixty-degree accession
of red eyed maroons escaping mainland regulation

Turn the tables, tread heavily on egg shell-shocked crusts
Crush the display cabinet asunder mantle pieced civilisation

She reveals masks to prove with Tamir Rice we stand together,
George Floyd, a march of millions, gather, unmentioned

The umpire at the Far-Right net court overrules
as she steps away and forward from the base line

and returns backhanded compliments,
with serving suggestions, whitewashed in noodle ads

The hawk-eyed surveillance capitalist cameras and chatrooms
are trained on her every flexing sinuous muscular movement

Markets highly strung, rackets and sponsorship dealings
silence lambs to slaughtered race relations

Yet, Naomi attempts a lob, a volley, a declaratory smash
that Black Lives Matter.

Outcasts

Burakumin Meat Market

Hate mail cradles the tabletop
Medieval prejudice sharpens
Poison penned lettering
Festering marbled meat, flies on beef

Burakumin bells, albatross around their necks
Spell unclean, untouchable slaughtered men
poison penned at the abattoir
Fortunes diced whilst fatty wagyu ribbons slice

Craftsmanship butchered by secrets
Names written on buraku lists
Butterflies pinned under glass ceilings
Suffocating beneath a feudal pyramid

They wear their clinical scrubs smeared red
Collars up like Dracula awaiting their fate
lips dressed in cynical smiles inherited
Hamlet people remain segregated

Tainted by death at the fatty edges
Impure, their own executioners, undertakers.

Eta

Caste out Eta in our excrement
kegare sevenths sliced people
sink in the dirty water
Still, they are written off, filthy
lettered, animal liberation first
Eta accused of slaughter.

III

Yamaguchi-gumi

Within miasma's lingering stigma
Into the bosom of yakuza they run
Sheltering within family, discipline
Housed in unknown meritocracy
Pledge loyalty to the boss of the mob.

Gomi

Complicated garbage systems for citizens
Each city, town and district is shrouded in mystery
Trash separation coloured by numbers: pamphlets,
notices and signs; (non) combustibles, recyclables
or oversized out of date dream spectacles
scheduled for public collection

Gaijin ants teem in piles, termite trash mounds
cash strapped scavengers seek lost and found
in rising yen mountains, consumer goods cornucopias
Jettisoned from upwardly mobile apartment blocks
Ballast for the masses as the sky is scraped utopian
Treasures sit high on concrete slabs, found and lost.

All Wrapped Up

Sushi dresses in sequined seaweed jackets
Treats in separate bowls double wrapped
Lunches packed in lacquered black
Bento box elegance
Japanese sweets swaddled Russian dolls

Unravel the everyday layers
Of giri gift giving duties,
outside clues enamelled
the nail that stands up must be hammered
to what lies inside, prise it open
Humans wrapped in history, rigid
dress codes still in vogue

An obi bow ties up the present
Legs and torsos trussed uncomfortably
A geisha group in mummified huddle
Kimono presents of the past,
Past and present collide and elide

Salarymen studded by enamel
in midnight blue suits, pinstriped by shooting stars
seppuku stabbed by honorific badges
Butterflies trapped in glass;
lapel pins fade and lose their twinkle.

Bata Kusai

Red-haired, blue-eyed goblins
Garble Japlish garbed in hot woollen clothes
swaddle sweaty bodies. Alien, friend or foe?
View the ill-bathed hirsute anatomy
Pegged haughty noses expose bata kusai

The butter stinking,
fatty animal eaters
How can't they match our fastidious standards?
Add the inventory, the list of noxious,
Obnoxious Occidental things:

Portuguese in the sixteenth,
Americans in the nineteenth
Our post-war wonderment turns to revulsion
when Black GIs show their true skin
In splendid isolation's mirror

Unconsciously, we side with whites
in sixties civil rights, movements and marches
Now JET-black repulsion and fear of refugees
southwards, racial narratives run deep.

A New Frame - Commemorative Photos

They organise in the rows
serried behind the tripod
Dotted arrangements assemble
Thames side and by Parliament
SNAP! The kinen shashin,

our momentous photos
Line up in homogenous monochrome
Before the polaroid pixels vanish, mercurial
as quick and silvery as it arrives
step aside the quicksand

before the picture explodes in rainbow tones
The divide between subject and object erodes;
Uchi and soto on a smartphone photo
Out of the ghetto, out of splendid isolation
In the lightning flash lose consciousness

Lose your self-image, pure privileges
Unbind the myth, untie the shoe-laced legends
that bind race, culture and nation in a close-knit system
Them and us inseparable from the gaijin.

Tremor & Remember

Tremor and remember
Somersault and spin bodies gripped like yo-yos
puppets on umbilical strings
developing in utero

Tremor and remember
Kalahari keepers of n/om, shake
Smear symbols in ochred Blombos caves
Rock, sing, dance and sway

Tremor and remember
Each arm held upright
crucified in shaking discharge
The resurrection by Swahili midwives

Tremor and remember
Meditate until you shake
The life force striking seiki jitsu
Zen Samurai superhumans preparing for earthquake
Tremor and remember
Tremor and forget.

Kintsugi Kente

weave kintsugi kente strips
stitch us strong from broken places
made from one cloth
our lacquer shines beyond
mountainous Maroon ridges
seamless golden threaded rivers
connect coastal embedded memories

together tapestry estrangement
an alchemy in melting pots and cauldrons
mix powdered gold, silver and platinum
our ancestors before us
run fingertips along keloid skin
ridged twice strong through thick and thin

cast off the bandages and shackles
to reveal our kansha good and bad
mushin illuminates our frailty, everchanging
cracks across Black Atlantic Ocean flaws
the seas embed triangular enslavement
lost in Bermuda, Brazil, Barbados
yet our third eye remains open, hopeful
lacquered and attached in seamless overlap

in waves kintsugi kente weaves its gold and stretches
blue veins ripple and oxygenate you
as we breathe in subaqueous empires beneath
Drexciyan dreams come true
Anansi spins a capoeira carapace
silky strings twist and gyrate healing nations
in double helix mystery, limbo defying moves
resist the holds of slave ships, we wriggle out

of their grip and shapeshift
along tribal scars and fault lines guide us
colluding chiefs, governments and massas
heals rifts in transatlantic valleys forever
to lineages that coruscate their treasure
join cracks with piece methods and joint calls
to arms in action, in each fissure flowers a vision
sit on the golden stool and raise up the palanquin
play magical balafon, gourd vibrations amplified
on twenty-one imperial leather kora strings

each break etches complex journeys
nourish us as each piece meets, our creole tongues
clutch palates, grip hybrid linguistic staffs
and speak new visions, one yuimara value
vulnerable yet strong,
praise Onyankopon, the kami, our gods.

Clover Haibun

Trefoil Trinity
connecting landscapes threefold
in shifting seasons,

any given space
poems and prose plant themselves
without entrenchment

Leave whispered postscripts
prosaic introductions
until journey's end

Murmuring meaning
wood block text rectangular
stands, stir haiku bowls

Flags signpost neatly
Basho's *aware*
travels without getting lost.

Travel in the Direction of Your Fear

We must travel in the direction of our fears – John Berryman

Travels in Japan like a shinkansen
A bullet through unseen trajectories
A twenty something exchanging worlds
swapping the west for eastern fantasies
On an oriental adventure
A hatsumode arrow, shooting
skywards, now the past is remembered
hinomaru rising son of futures

Suddenly free! We're outmanoeuvring
old prejudices and identities
jettisoned ballast every day and mundane
No longer the exotic destination
Travelling in the direction of fear
Arriving at a place forever held dear.

Notes

'The Illogical Progressions – Lab Rats in Roppongi' borrows language from 'Planetary Funk Alert' Track 7 of 'Progression Sessions 1' by LTJ Bukem featuring MC Conrad

Acknowledgements

Grateful acknowledgment is made to the editors and staff of the following anthology, in which a version of 'Blossom' originally appeared: *Red Penguin Books*
'Blossom' appeared in *the flower shop on the corner*, edited by JK Larkin, 2021

www.ingramcontent.com/pod-product-compliance
Lightning Source LLC
Chambersburg PA
CBHW051721040426
42446CB00032B/1136